W. K. KELLOGG FUND

W9-ARZ-772

The FIRST BOOK of
CONSERVATION

J
353.72
S

SBN 531-00510-0

The author's thanks to Dr. Ira N. Gabrielson,
President, Wildlife Management Institute, for
his helpful suggestions regarding the manu-
script of this book.

18 19 20

Library of Congress Catalog Card Number: 54-5987
Printed in the United States of America by The Garrison Corp.
Published in Canada by Ambassador Books Ltd., Toronto 1, Ontario

THE FIRST BOOK OF
Conservation

By F. C. SMITH

Pictures by RENE MARTIN

FRANKLIN WATTS, INC.
575 LEXINGTON AVENUE
NEW YORK 22, N. Y.

Copyright 1954 by Franklin Watts, Inc.

GIVING AND TAKING

THOUSANDS of kinds of plants, insects, birds, fish, reptiles and animals, and over two billion human beings inhabit this earth. Each kind is in many ways different from every other kind. A mosquito is not much like a grizzly bear or a man. The tiny blue mold on a loaf of old bread is not much like a huge oak or a giant redwood tree. Yet they are all living things. And in one way they are alike: they all depend on the work of other living things in order to stay alive themselves. Every single one takes something from other living things and from some non-living things, too. And every single one gives something, also.

All growing green plants take minerals from the soil. Many of these minerals actually came to the soil from decayed plants and animals. For when wild plants and animals die they give something back to the earth.

The growing trees give homes to birds—and birds help the trees by eating insects which might damage them.

All through nature there is a constant giving and taking, although, of course, plants, insects, fish, birds, reptiles and animals do not carefully plan this out. They simply live naturally and without thinking as they use what they need from other living things and from soil, water, air and sunlight. It is a way of life that has developed over millions of years.

The whole delicately related system of living things rests on the broad foundation of green plants. Without green plants nothing else could survive. People can build great cities. They can make airplanes that fly at terrific speed. But they cannot use nature's raw materials to make their own food inside their bodies. Only green plants can do this. They make not only their own food but food for every other living thing on earth. Many forms of life, like cattle, rabbits and squirrels, are plant-eaters. Others, like foxes and hawks, eat the flesh of plant-eaters. People depend on the flesh of plant-eaters for meat.

Green plants, with the help of sunlight, air, water and minerals from the soil, are wonderful food factories. From the air they take a gas, carbon dioxide. From the soil they take water. With the help of the green coloring matter in their leaves, called "chlorophyll," they somehow trap the energy of sunlight and use it with the carbon dioxide and water in their leaves to produce a form of sugar. This is food for the plants.

From the soil plants also take minerals. By adding these to the sugar they have made they form other food containing fats, proteins and carbohydrates. These fats, proteins and carbohydrates, in fruits, vegetables, stems, roots and leaves, are food for other living things. The plant process of using sunlight, carbon dioxide and water to make food is called "photosynthesis," which means "putting together by means of light." Scientists have been studying photosynthesis for years, but they do not yet completely understand it.

In nature's great exchange, green plants give back something to both air and soil. Plants take in more oxygen than they need for making food, so, though we cannot see it, they put back oxygen into the air each day. Animals breathe the oxygen and in turn give back to the air carbon dioxide, which the plants use. Plants help, too, in keeping the air moist. Their roots take water from the soil. What the plants do not use goes into the air from their leaves as water vapor.

9

Plants also drop leaves, which make a spongelike surface on the ground. This soaks up rain water which might otherwise run off. Plants' roots keep the soil from packing hard, and air and water follow the roots' tunnels into the earth. Roots also help hold the soil so that it does not wash away in heavy rains. Look at a plant root sometime and see how its many tiny fibers cling to the soil.

Oxygen and air moisture, and help in keeping the ground in good condition—all these things green plants give in return for what they take from earth and air.

There is a giving and taking also between green plants and some of the non-green plants called "fungi" and "bacteria." Have you ever seen a toadstool in your yard, mushrooms growing out of a rotting tree stump, or mold on cheese or bread? These are some of the many forms of fungi. Perhaps you have seen swellings on the roots of sweet clover. These are made by some kinds of bacteria.

Fungi and many bacteria cannot make their own food, for they have no chlorophyll. They must take their food from

10

living or dead plant and animal material. Single bacteria are too small to be seen without a microscope. But millions and millions of them live all around us on animals or other plants, in soil or air. A scientist has said that an acre of rich farmland can feed three 30-pound woodchucks, but the same acre of land can support 240 pounds of bacteria and another 240 pounds of fungi and animals as tiny as bacteria.

In taking their food from old or dead plant and animal matter, bacteria and fungi cause decay. This means that they constantly change the plant and animal matter on which they live into simpler and simpler chemicals. Gradually the chemicals go back into the air in the form of carbon dioxide and other gases or into the soil in forms which living green plants can use to make food.

So bacteria and fungi greatly help other kinds of life. If decay did not take place, all the carbon dioxide in the air would probably be used up in about forty years. Most of the nitrogen and other important chemicals in the soil would disappear also. Green plants depend on bacteria and fungi to help furnish the chemicals which they need in making food for the world.

THE WORK OF INSECTS

A FAMOUS insect scientist has said that there are one hundred times as many *kinds* of insects in the world as there are single stars which you can see in the sky—and those are countless. Insects seem to be everywhere in the world around us. They are different from most other animal life because they go through several forms as they grow. A baby deer or rabbit looks something like its parents, but a butterfly, for example, was once a caterpillar. The lives of the millions of insects in all their forms are closely bound up with plants. Plants provide food for most kinds of insects, at least when they are young. Caterpillars, cutworms, grubs, beetles, grasshoppers, aphids and many others eat leaves, stems, plant juices or roots. Bees, butterflies and young wasps use nectar, the sweet juice of flowers, for making food. And some insects devour the insects which are plant-eaters.

Plants furnish homes for many insects. Twenty thousand tiny plant lice, or aphids, may live on one tree. A young praying mantis makes its home in a bush on the underside of a branch, and many caterpillars do, also. Tent caterpillars build white webs in wild cherries or other trees. Some insects hide their eggs in little bumps on leaves or stems of plants until they hatch. Even wasps use wood from plants to make the paper with which they build their homes.

Many insects can hide themselves perfectly on plants, and so find protection from enemies. Green aphids or grasshoppers can scarcely be seen against leaves and stems. The insect called a walking stick looks almost exactly like a brown twig.

But insects help plants, too. Without them, many plants could not pro-

duce fruits or some of our common vegetables. In fact, without help from bees, moths and butterflies, some green plants would disappear from the earth. This is why: Within flowers is a fine yellow dust called "pollen." In order to form seeds and produce more flowers and fruit from year to year, plants must pass this pollen from blossom to blossom. But flowers have no way of carrying pollen. Wind blows some of it from one blossom to another, but not all plants are able to catch wind-borne pollen. Insects carry the pollen of some kinds of plants directly from one blossom to another.

A bee lights on a flower to draw nectar from it and also to gather pollen, both of which it uses in making food. As the bee clings to the flower, yellow pollen sticks to the fine hairs of its legs and body. As the bee flies from blossom to blossom to draw more nectar, pollen from one flower rubs off on other flowers. So pollen spreads, making it possible for flowers to form fruit and seeds and produce new plants. Bees are by far the most important insect carriers of pollen. Some large fruit-growers keep honeybee hives in their orchards so that the bees will work there to keep the orchards bearing fruit each season.

Termites are tiny, antlike insects which almost constantly chew wood. Inside the termites live even smaller animals which change the wood into chemicals that the termites can digest. Termites can chew so much wood from a fence or a set of porch steps, or sometimes even the walls of a building, that it will fall down. But in the forests termites give useful service. Termites and wood-eating beetles help plants like bacteria and fungi to break down all kinds of dead plant matter into chemicals which can be reused in the soil and air. Bodies of dead insects, especially ants, also help enrich the soil, returning chemicals to it.

Many insects are little plows, or even little bulldozers. Ants and beetles which live in the ground make tunnels and holes. These openings allow air and water to enter the soil and help plants to grow. Ants burrow energetically. They bring deep-down soil up nearer the top where it can receive chemicals and become fertile for raising more plants. Ants are small, but so numerous that they accomplish much.

When a robin sings outside your window, you can be glad that there are insects. Insects furnish food for thousands of birds and for other forms of life including spiders, toads, snakes and some four-footed animals.

They even furnish food for other insects. Ants get some food from the tiny plant lice called aphids. Ants do not eat these lice, but take from them a sweet liquid which the aphids make from plant juices that are their food. When an ant strokes an aphid with its feelers the aphid releases a drop of this sweet juice, called "honeydew." The ant drinks this or even stores it in its extra stomach to carry back to other ants in the burrow. The insects who do this work are called ant cowherds. They actually take care of the aphids, sometimes carry them to pasture from plant to plant, and fight off the aphids' insect enemies.

This ant-aphid combination may not seem good for people because aphids destroy some plants. But usually the work the ants do for the soil repays both plants and people.

From the point of view of human beings some insects are harmful and some are helpful. Insects don't purposely decide which to be. They merely do things naturally, in a way that enables them to go on living. Sometimes they eat the fruit or grain that farmers raise, or, like the malaria mosquito, they carry disease. Then men call them harmful. But many insect pests have developed because people have upset the natural relations of plant and insect life. And even though some insects are harmful at times they all play their important part in nature, where every living thing is connected in some way with other living things.

16

ANIMALS IN THE PLAN

BIRDS, fish, snakes and four-footed animals need plants. They need trees, shrubs and grasses for their homes, for protection from their enemies, and often for food. A squirrel builds a snug home in the trunk of a hollow hickory tree. It eats nuts, the fruit of the tree. When enemies come, it darts up the trunk of the tree and escapes.

A grass-eating rabbit is being chased by a coyote. Zigzagging over a pasture, it suddenly slips into a tangled briar patch where the coyote cannot follow.

A flock of wild ducks flies over a lake shore. Below them they see tall grasses and reeds, plants which offer food and protection. The ducks alight on the water among the reeds.

A fish, dining on insects, has its meal interrupted by an

otter, which wants to dine on a fish. Perhaps the fish can hide among a tangle of underwater plants.

And so it goes. Animal life constantly makes use of plants.

In turn, animal life does important jobs for plants. The oak or hickory tree where the squirrel has its home is, like most plants, unable to move to carry its seeds to new places for sowing. Birds and animals help plant life to spread. Squirrels and chipmunks store acorns and other nuts in the ground, sometimes forgetting to dig them up. These forgotten seeds stay in the earth and often grow into trees. Sometimes birds take seeds in their bills and fly away to eat them or carry them to their young. They drop some seeds accidentally. Seeds that are parts of berries, like mulberry and wild blackberry, are sometimes eaten by birds or animals, and pass through their bodies unharmed, as waste material. Some seeds are sticky or barbed, and cling to the bodies of birds and animals for a time until they fall off in new places. Sometimes a dog comes home with burs caught in its fur. In the same way that it sits down and scratches the burs out

18

on the lawn, a rabbit or raccoon scratches them out in woods or fields, so planting seeds in new spots. And hummingbirds help to pollinate flowers just as insects do.

Animals depend on insects, too. Snakes, toads, frogs, fish, raccoons, skunks and even bears use insects as part of their food.

Birds eat tremendous numbers of insects. Young birds in a nest have their mouths open most of the time because they are always hungry. Birds have their young in the summertime when plant food is abundant for insects. Because there are many insects at this time, young birds as well as parent birds also have plenty to eat.

The words "food chain" are used to describe the way in which two or more kinds of living things are linked to each other because they depend on one another for food. Of course, plants are the first link in every chain, but there are many, many different food chains. Hungry young birds eating millions of insects during the summer while insects are busily eating plants are links in only one food chain among thousands.

These are links in other food chains:

A small meadow mouse is chewing the roots of a young corn plant. It sticks its head out of its hole. Quick as a flash a red-tailed hawk swoops from the sky and grabs the mouse.

Between the rows of cotton on a Southern plantation, a strange-looking animal, an opossum, waddles along in the moonlight. It has come to hunt the cotton rat which eats the farmer's cotton plants.

In the warm ground of a Midwestern field, a six-foot-long bull snake crushes the life from a grass-eating gopher and swallows it for its meal.

20

Down along the wood-lot fence on a winter evening, a rabbit is eating the bark of a young tree. There's a sudden swift rush and the plant-eating rabbit has become food for a gray fox.

In those fields and woods there may have been too many mice, too many gophers and too many rabbits for their natural food supply, so that they used man's plants. By eating the extra, or surplus, numbers the hawk, the snake, the fox and the opossum were useful to people.

Even though some animals eat the grass in a farmer's meadow, or his cotton plants, or the young trees in his wood lot, their kind is useful to him in other ways. The holes and tunnels made by mice, gophers, moles, snakes, chipmunks and shrews carry air and water into the soil. The extra rabbits and mice furnish food for animals like foxes and coyotes and keep them from raiding the farmer's chicken pen. Each kind of animal has its place in nature's system.

NATURE'S SPECIALISTS

SOME wild creatures do very special jobs. Those which eat dead and decaying animal matter, called "carrion," serve as a clean-up crew. In the United States these animals include vultures, or buzzards, carrion beetles, and such part-time workers as eagles, crows, coyotes and bears, which eat carrion occasionally. These creatures help bacteria and fungi in keeping dead material from accumulating in too great amounts.

The beaver is an important specialist. He is an engineer who lives and works on streams. He swims to shore, waddles to a small tree, turns his head to one side and starts whittling big chips from the tree with his chisel-like front teeth. When the tree is cut down, he and his family drag pieces of it to the

22

water and use them, together with stones, sticks and mud, to build a dam which holds back water and makes a pond.

In the middle of the pond or in the dam the beavers build a house of sticks and mud. They store many logs in the bottom of the pond for their winter's supply of food, which is bark from trees. The pond makes a safe home for the beaver family. It provides homes, too, for other wild creatures such as muskrats, fish, ducks and geese.

Beaver ponds help prevent floods, too. For when the waters from spring rains and melting snows rush downstream, beaver dams slow them up and make them spread out. This gives time for the soil carried along by the floodwaters to settle to the bottom of the pond. There is time, too, for much of the water to soak deep into nature's underground water-storage places.

After the beavers have eaten the bark from the trees near their pond they move to a new location. The old dam gradu-

23

ally breaks and the pond dries up, leaving a meadow of rich soil. Many of the beautiful parklike meadows in the Rocky Mountains and small rich fields in the East and South grew from old beaver ponds.

The earthworm is a specialist that not everyone appreciates. Earthworms take their main food supply from leaves and other plant matter on top of the ground. They usually feed at night, when some of them are caught as "night-crawlers" for fish bait. But the important work of earthworms is soil cultivation. To make its home, an earthworm burrows in the ground and swallows the soil as it digs. It digests some food from the soil and passes the rest through its body, leaving it at the top of its burrow. This soil is ground fine by going through the worm's body, and it is made rich by body juices. Scientists have found that in some places earthworms have gradually covered rocky ground with soil. The burrowing of worms also lets air and water into the ground. Without the help of earthworms as soil conditioners, some places on our earth would not produce plants well.

In all these ways and in thousands and thousands of others the lives of plants, insects and animals are bound up with each other and with man. Without thinking or planning, but by leading their natural lives, these wild things of the earth give and take from each other. They help our world produce the things we all need.

People have not always realized how much they depend on the natural working of all living things. In the United States we have always used all the things of nature, particularly the forests, the grass, the animals, and the soil and water which support them. We have called these things part of our natural resources and thought of them as some of our own wealth and our country's wealth. For years it seemed as if there were so many plants and animals and so much water and soil that we would always have all we needed. Until recently we have not paid much attention to the "give and take" of all natural things. We have *taken*, but we have forgotten that every living thing, including human beings, must also *give* in order to survive.

The actions of people have important effects on other people and on all forms of nature. Scientists have begun to study these effects. They realize that people have damaged the earth so badly that we must work to save our natural resources. They are trying to learn how we can live with all things on earth and still not harm their relationships.

The study of the relationships of everything in nature is called "ecology." The scientists called "ecologists" are thinking about the way our country used to be and the way it is now. They know that some things in nature have changed for the worse, and they know why. But they are finding that it is often hard to know how to make these things better again.

OUR COUNTRY LONG AGO

IF YOU had been an Indian boy or girl in the days before white men came to North America, you would have seen a land far different from that of today. Almost all the Eastern part of the country as well as much of the vast mountain region of the West was covered with great forests. To walk in one of these was to be in a strange and beautiful world. A springy carpet of dead leaves lay always on the ground. The air was cool and moist. The largest trees were very old. Their tops made a deep shade, but between some of the great trees sunlight sifted down to where young trees, saplings and seedlings grew crowded together as they reached upward for light.

26

The animals, reptiles, insects, birds, fish and plants that lived in these untouched forests or in the open spaces at their edges furnished food for each other. Each had its place in nature's scheme, from the insects up to the large, graceful deer that browsed on the bushes and the lower branches of the trees, so trimming them and helping the saplings and seedlings to get the air and sunshine they needed to grow into sturdy trees. Even wolves and panthers had a part to play, for they ate the surplus deer and so kept them from destroying too many plants. By killing the weaker deer, wolves and panthers kept the deer herds healthy, also.

When one of the old trees began to die, insects and wood-peckers bored holes in it so that rain water and air hastened its breakdown. Fungi in lovely delicate colors grew on the tree, holding moisture which softened the wood. When the tree fell, the fungi and bacteria continued their work. The wood softened still more and crumbled into the soil. In this way the dead trees returned to the soil and air all the chemicals which they had taken in growing. In turn, the enriched soil gave food and life to new seedlings.

This way of life had gone on for many thousands of years. Trees and other plants grew and fell, grew and fell, and provided homes and food for other living things.

Between the forested lands of East and West were the Great Plains, stretching from the Mississippi Valley to the Rocky Mountains. Here was a different kind of land. There were few trees, but the vast rolling prairie was covered with thick grass. Here, just as in the forests, plants, animals, fish, insects and birds furnished food for one another. Some were grass-eaters such as deer, elks, antelopes, buffaloes and many small ground animals — rabbits, prairie dogs and mice. Others like the wolves and coyotes ate the flesh of the grass-eaters.

In the forests and grasslands the streams ran pure and clear. The Indians were spread so widely over the vast forests and prairies that what they took from the plants and animals each year was usually replaced by the following year's natural growth. Even though disease or drought might sometimes change the numbers of plants or animals in one place, the effect was not widespread over the country.

WHAT HAPPENED

BEGINNING with the latter part of the sixteenth century, white men settled in North America. In about three hundred years they made more changes than there had been for perhaps thousands of years before. These white men were mostly farming people, who brought axes and plows. With their tools they felled thousands of acres of forest trees and plowed up the green lands to plant crops like wheat and corn. These crops covered the soil for only a few months of the year. In between growing seasons the ground was left bare. Sometimes, in clearing the land for crops, the early settlers did not even bother to cut the trees, but burned them instead. It seemed

30

to these people that there were far too many trees growing.

It is true that the white men made some of these changes so that they could survive, since some of the grass and tree land had to be planted with grain to feed the increasing numbers of people. But often the changes were carelessly made.

Hundreds of forests on the hills and slopes were cut down.

Thousands of acres of grasslands were plowed up for planting grain. On the remaining grass and forest lands ranchers sometimes let too many sheep and cattle graze. There was not enough food for them all, and the animals cropped the grass and bushes too close. When these things happened, the earth was left without its natural blanket of plants, called its "plant cover."

31

Too often, when their land had been worn away, or "eroded," by wind and water, the farmers did nothing to repair the damage. They merely moved westward to new acres, until the day came when much of the empty territory was occupied.

As cities grew up, there was great need for lumber. Sometimes lumbermen greedy for money cut all the trees in a forest, leaving no way of providing seeds for new growths. Or sometimes careless men allowed forest fires to start by dropping lighted matches or failing to put out campfires. Often, in a few days, forest fires wiped out thousands of acres of trees that had taken years to grow.

In destroying the forests and plowing up the grass, men removed too much plant cover from the "watersheds" of our country. A watershed is any ridge and its slopes down which rain water or melting snow can run into a stream or pond, a marsh or lake. A natural watershed may be a little thing like the sides of a ditch or a brook, or it may be as large as the slopes of the Continental Divide in the Rocky Mountains, in some places over 14,000 feet high. The water on the east side of the Continental Divide flows toward the Atlantic Ocean, and on the west side toward the Pacific Ocean. But there are thousands of smaller watersheds on both sides.

If you have a spot of earth to dig in, you can make a model watershed by building a hill and a valley with a stream in it. If you pack down the bare earth on your hill, then pour water from a sprinkling can over it until the earth is soaked, much soil will wash away. If you pull grass and leaves and cover your hill with them beforehand, however, not so much water and earth are carried into the stream.

The grass and leaves are plant cover for your tiny hill. On nature's watersheds plant cover works in this same way. If you have ever upset a glass of milk or water on a table with a cloth and pad on it, you know how the liquid soaked into them. You know, however, that if the table had been bare a good deal of the liquid would have run to the edge and spilled onto the floor. In the same way that the cloth and pad blotted up the moisture, trees and grass, with their thick roots and their leaves, help water to soak into the ground where it is needed, instead of running off rapidly and taking soil with it.

Perhaps you remember rainstorms so hard that they washed the dirt from the flower bed or driveway into the street. But where the grass was thick on the lawn the dirt did not wash away. Or you have walked through woods after a rain and have seen how every dead leaf on the ground was a tiny cup that held a few drops of rain water. Plant covers were working there.

As more and more grass and trees were removed from our country's watersheds, there was not enough natural plant cover to slow up the runoff of water on the slopes. Even on level ground, crops like corn, wheat and cotton, which cover the earth for only part of the year, did not protect the land as well as the forest trees and grass had done. Trees and grass had been a plant cover whose roots held the earth the year round and prevented the rich topsoil from washing off in heavy rains and blowing away in hot dry winds.

Gradually floods became worse. There have always been some seasonal floods, but as the years went by they grew more frequent and damaging. In the former grasslands of the Midwest, great dust storms came in the times of little rain. Sometimes the air was so thick with dust that day seemed as dark as night. The rich topsoil was blowing off the fields.

Garbage and sewage from the cities that grew up rapidly as our country developed were often dumped into the streams. This made the water unfit for fish, animals or people to use. Waste matter from factories and mines was poured into streams, also.

Gradually, over the years, as all these things happened to the forests, the grass, the land and the waters, the results began to ruin plant and animal life and to harm people. Besides floods and dust storms, there were water shortages and crop failures. Plants could not grow well in the poor soil left when the topsoil disappeared. Many experts even say there is danger of future food shortages in our rich nation, just as there have been in other, older nations which have been careless of their natural resources.

What the white men on this continent had done was to upset the natural relationships of living things. For, just as all living things are affected by each other, they are also affected by their surroundings. And in turn they affect their surroundings, or what we call their "environment." Natural surroundings are called "natural environment." White men had changed their natural environment too rapidly.

If you go on a trip, sometimes even a short trip, you will often see several different kinds of natural environment. You may see woods, open fields, creeks, bare rocky hilltops and swamps. These are all little natural communities. You can think of others.

There are seas, marshes, lakes, streams, forests, mountains and deserts, and grasslands without trees. The kinds of natural environment differ according to the change in climate, amount of rainfall, kind of soil, altitude and the lay of the land—whether it is hilly, flat or something in between.

Each kind of environment has certain kinds of plants and animals which are especially suited to living in those surroundings. Even though many kinds of animals and plants have a wide range over several regions, others can live in only one kind of environment. You would never expect to see a heavily furred polar bear in the jungle or a warmth-loving alligator on the arctic ice. You look for squirrels among nut trees, and prairie dogs on the prairie. You never see a cactus plant in a marsh, or cattails in a desert. Plants of the cactus family are especially suited to dry desert air because they have hard wax surfaces which prevent the sun from evaporating their moisture. Marsh plants like cattails have masses of long roots which hold them in the watery soil.

When an environment is changed, that affects the living things within it. If the moist soil of a certain place is made dry, as it might be if a man drains the water from a marsh, the plants that grow in wet soil can no longer live there, nor can the birds and animals, such as ducks or muskrats, that depend on the water plants for food and protection. If for some reason the trees and shrubs that are the homes of insect-eating birds are cut down and the birds have no shelter, they must go elsewhere. Then the insects in that place may grow too numerous and become pests.

Upsetting the relationships of nature has had most serious effects, sometimes direct and sometimes indirect, on our natural resources of soil, water, and plant and animal life. The changes and disturbances made by the white men on this continent have affected the lives of all of us.

CONSERVATION AT WORK

WHEN ecologists began to realize that careless, wasteful methods of farming and industry were changing the natural environment too rapidly and destroying our resources, they went to work. They began to plan how to renew our soil, our forests and grasslands and our wildlife. The work of *managing* these and our mineral resources wisely is called "conservation." People who help conservation are "conservationists." Everyone can and should be a conservationist. A boy or girl who plants a needed tree, puts out birdhouses, or saves a useful plant or animal life is a conservationist.

There are, however, conservation *specialists* who are showing the way to work with nature wisely. They are trying to

39

decide what each natural environment is best suited for. They have learned that in some regions of scant rainfall and thin soil, like parts of our Western states, it is wise to leave the land in grass as food for the right number of beef cattle rather than to plow up the grass and plant grain. They know also that a marsh is not necessarily waste land simply because no corn, wheat or cotton is growing on it. For a marsh can be a valuable soil-builder and water-holder, important to the country's water supply.

Conservationists are helping farmers to see that in order to grow any food crop successfully the environment must be right for that crop. Scientists in our national and state governments, in our agricultural schools and on our farms are constantly experimenting to find out how to use the land best. Gradually farmers are learning to build up their land by planting crops that will help it instead of those that will bring in quick money for a few seasons, then leave the soil useless and ruined.

Conservationists help farmers in ways like this: In the Midwest a few years ago a farmer named Bill Anderson was worried. For several years he had not earned as much money from his crops as he should have. He looked over his washed-away fields and he realized that if something was not done soon, in a few years he would have no farm.

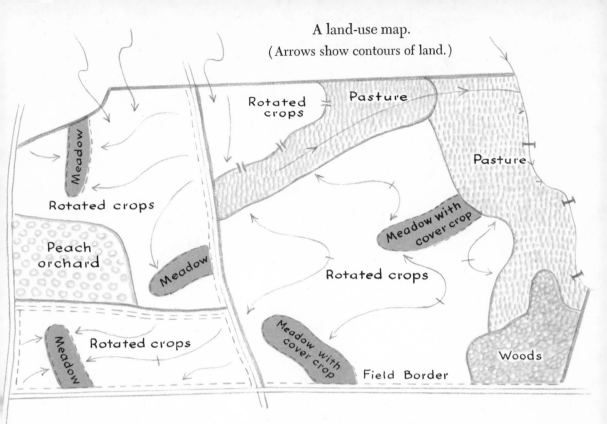

A land-use map.
(Arrows show contours of land.)

He wrote to his County Agricultural Bureau and to the United States Soil Conservation Service for help with his problem. A conservation specialist came to see Bill Anderson. He took samples of soil from various parts of Bill's farm and sent them to a laboratory. There experts found out what soil chemicals the samples contained. Then the conservation specialist made a sketch of the whole farm, showing the different kinds of slopes, hills, flatlands and soil. Together he and Bill made a "land-use map" and decided what the various parts of the farm were best suited for and how they should be used.

Then Bill Anderson went to work. Some fields were suited only for pasture. These he left in grass. Others he cultivated in special ways to protect the land and also to restore valuable chemicals to the worn-out soil. This was done by rotating crops—that is, by planting crops like clover or soy beans which restore nitrogen to the soil, then plowing them under and planting grain which needs the nitrogen. In his cornfields Bill plowed his furrows across the slope instead of down it. This plowing to follow the natural curves or "contours" of the land made each furrow into a little dam which held back water and kept it from washing away the rich topsoil. On some slopes Bill made terraces to hold the water. On others he left strips of sod between the plowed sections. Where deep gullies had been worn he built little dams, and in the smaller ditches he planted grass. He planted trees and shrubs along the muddy creek banks. In some fence rows he planted hedges as homes for insect-eating birds and game animals.

42

After a few years Bill Anderson had nature working *with* him on his farm. He had helped to control floods. His study of conservation had paid off in better crops and valuable wildlife. And if Bill Anderson, and his neighbors, will continue to work wisely on their precious acres they will continue to have the good crops that we all need.

Men are learning how to help nature correct the damage done to our forests, too. When lumber is cut, whether in a farmer's wood lot or in a great forest, enough trees should be left standing to provide seed for new trees and to furnish shade for the protection of young seedlings from strong sun and wind and from weeds. In our national forests and in some privately owned forests, trees are now cut in this way.

In some areas where already too many trees have been cut or burned away, young trees must be transplanted from a nursery. Many of our state governments, our national government and some private companies have tree nurseries where

tree seeds are planted. Then the seedlings are cared for until they are strong enough to be transplanted to a natural environment. Foresters, farmers, school children or anyone else interested can often buy seedling trees for a few cents each and plant them where they are needed. If your school or club wants to plant trees, write for information to your state Department of Forestry or Department of Agriculture at the state capital.

Another way to build up our woodlands is to provide shelter for nature's own tree-planters—squirrels, chipmunks, birds and other animals.

In our nation, besides twenty-six national parks, there are about 160 national forests with an area of over 229 million acres—and hundreds of state forests. These are set aside not only to prevent a shortage of wood but also to make sure that enough trees are left to protect the important watersheds of our country. Citizens must watch that thoughtless people do not pass laws which would take these forests from the protection of the various forestry departments and allow them to be cut wastefully.

NATIONAL PARKS AND NATIONAL FOREST AREAS

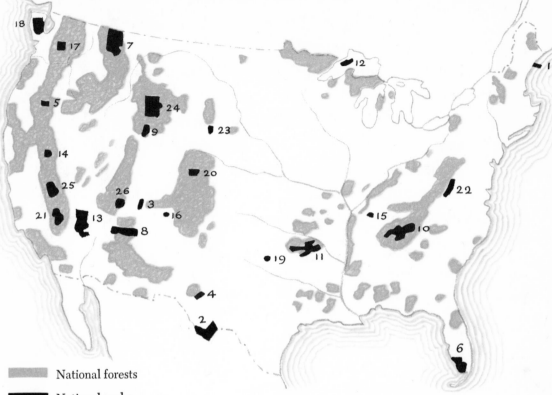

National forests

National parks

National parks are listed below. The year of each park's establishment is in parentheses.

1. Acadia, Maine (1919), 29,978 acres.
2. Big Bend, Texas (1944), 692,305 acres.
3. Bryce Canyon, Utah (1928), 36,010 acres.
4. Carlsbad Caverns, New Mexico (1930), 45,846 acres.
5. Crater Lake, Oregon (1902), 160,290 acres.
6. Everglades, Florida (1947), 1,258,361 acres.
7. Glacier, Montana (1910), 999,015 acres.
8. Grand Canyon, Arizona (1919), 645,296 acres.
9. Grand Teton, Wyoming (1929), 299,580 acres.
10. Great Smoky Mountains, North Carolina and Tennessee (1930), 507,159 acres.
11. Hot Springs, Arkansas (1921), 1,019 acres.
12. Isle Royale, Michigan (1940), 133,839 acres.
13. Kings Canyon, California (1940), 453,065 acres.
14. Lassen Volcanic, California (1916), 103,809 acres.
15. Mammoth Cave, Kentucky (1936), 50,696 acres.
16. Mesa Verde, Colorado (1906), 51,018 acres.
17. Mount Rainier, Washington (1899), 241,571 acres.
18. Olympic, Washington (1938), 887,987 acres.
19. Platt, Oklahoma (1906), 912 acres.
20. Rocky Mountain, Colorado (1915), 245,736 acres.
21. Sequoia, California (1890), 385,138 acres.
22. Shenandoah, Virginia (1935), 193,473 acres.
23. Wind Cave, South Dakota (1903), 27,886 acres.
24. Yellowstone, Wyoming, Montana and Idaho (1872), 2,213,207 acres.
25. Yosemite, California (1890), 757,617 acres.
26. Zion, Utah (1919), 94,241 acres.

In addition, there are Hawaii National Park (1916), 176,951 acres on the island of Hawaii, and Mount McKinley National Park (1917), 1,939,319 acres in Alaska.

Perhaps this is most important of all: *We must keep our forests from burning.* Each year fire is the greatest destroyer of our remaining natural forests. Forest fires destroy not only the trees themselves but often burn and scorch the soil so that seeds may not be able to grow for five or six years, or perhaps ever again.

The United States Forest Service makes these suggestions for preventing forest fires. You and your friends, your parents and your teachers can help by following them carefully:

Be sure that your match is out. Break it in two before you throw it away.

Be sure that pipe ashes, cigarettes or cigars are dead before they are thrown away. This means even when traveling in a car.

Build a safe campfire. Scrape away all leaves, grass or pine needles from a spot five feet wide. Keep your fire small. *Never* build it against a tree or log or near brush.

Do not leave a fire untended.

Put out your fire completely when you leave. Soak the coals with water. Turn small sticks and drench both sides. Wet the ground around the fire. Be sure the last spark is dead.

Know the fire laws in your state. Learn the areas where campfire building is allowed, and get a fire-building permit if that is necessary.

Never burn leaves or brush in windy weather or when there is the slightest danger that the fire will get away.

Report any fire you discover. Go to the nearest telephone and ask for the local Fire Warden or Forest Ranger.

46

Conservationists are working with our water supply, also. In the valley of the Tennessee River are big dams. In the Colorado River in Arizona and Nevada is Lake Mead, 115 miles long, made by Hoover Dam, 726 feet high. In the Missouri River Basin is Fort Peck Dam, an earth-filled dam 250 feet high and 21,026 feet long, making a lake about 189 miles long. These big dams and lakes show how experts are trying to manage the water supply so that it can be used when and where it is needed. The dams are designed for several uses. They can provide water power to make electricity. The water they store can irrigate dry lands and can be used by cities. It is hoped, too, that they and others to be built will control floods. Not all the specialists are agreed

about this last purpose, however. Some say the best place to stop floods is before they become floods — along the watersheds of *all* the streams. They say the big dams cost too much and that in the Midwest especially the lakes will be filled with soil particles within fifty years or so, because there still is not enough plant cover on the watersheds. Perhaps the best way to stop floods may be some combination of all methods.

But two things seem certain now. Men need to study our water problems more, and men must work *with* nature, not against her. This means that soil and forest conservation are very important.

Nature has its own storage places for water — in underground streams and pools and in the soil itself. Underground streams coming to the surface make our natural springs. Wells are dug by drilling into the ground until an underground pool or stream is struck. Such pools and streams and the permanent dampness of the soil itself hold more water than all the creeks, brooks, rivers, lakes and man-made reservoirs on the surface of the earth.

When rain water falls on the ground, some of it runs down the surface slopes and some of it sinks into the soil. When the rain stops, the sun and wind go to work evaporating moisture, drawing it up into the air to make clouds of it again. They take moisture not only from the soil's surface but from the first few feet of earth beneath.

But part of the rain that fell has gone many feet down into the earth. The warmth and movement of the air on the surface usually do not evaporate it before enough clouds have formed for more rain to fall. That moisture far below the surface joins with water already deep in the ground. The top level of this water stored in the ground is called the "water table." This line, or water table, may be a few feet or many feet below the surface, depending on the kind of soil, the plant cover, the slope of the land and the amount of rainfall.

The amount of water stored in the ground is found by measuring how far below the surface the water table is. When the water table is low, there is less water in the ground and men have to dig deeper to find moisture. This may be because little rain has fallen, because men have used too much water, or because too much water has run off the surface instead of sinking into the ground.

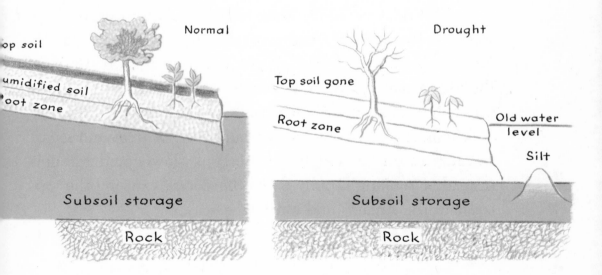

The underground water supply is like money in the bank. We draw on it for many things. Men drill wells in the ground and draw out water for farms and cities. Plant roots take moisture from underground water. Without it, men's crops could not produce food in times of little rain. But like money in the bank, if more is taken out than is put in the supply gets lower and lower.

The population of our country is increasing all the time, and so are the ways in which we use water. Air conditioning is a recent new use for it. Many modern factories need much water in their manufacturing work. More and more people are drawing on the water supply, either directly or through the use of more plants for food. We must help nature keep the underground storage tanks filled to their natural level.

We must provide plenty of plant cover, of trees and grass, to catch raindrops and help them sink slowly underground instead of running rapidly down the slopes, carrying the topsoil into the streams and out to the seas.

50

Conservationists are working to learn the best ways of managing insect life, too. Like all other living things, insects grow in greater or less numbers according to the food supply they can find. A meadow or woodland supplies food for fewer insects of one kind than the same land in grain. When men began to change woods and grasslands into great fields of cultivated grains and vegetables, insects which ate these became so numerous that they were a pest. Grasshoppers sometimes stripped cornfields of leaves. Chinch bugs ate the wheat crops. Potato bugs feasted on acres of potato plants, boll weevils destroyed cotton, and borers grew plentifully in apple orchards. We are still trying to find ways of keeping some insects in check and using the help of others.

Have you ever heard the roar of an airplane and looked up to see a daring pilot flying back and forth dangerously low over a field or orchard? That was a crop-duster. The cloud of dust shooting from his plane was a chemical to kill insects that were damaging valuable crops. Other ways of killing insects are by trapping them, destroying their breeding grounds, and by using their natural enemies.

51

Spraying poison is the most common way of killing insects, and it is sometimes a good way in cultivated fields and orchards. But farmers must be careful in the use of poisons. For they may also kill off too many of the insect pests' natural enemies, such as insect-eating birds, toads or fish.

People think that little good can be said for mosquitoes. Indeed, in the arctic regions during summer and in some other places they are a dangerous pest, and in the tropics one kind carries the disease malaria. Yet mosquitoes in both the young and grown-up stages furnish food for many kinds of fish and birds, particularly for waterfowl in northern lakes and marshes, and for rare birds and valuable fish in southern and coastal swamps. In controlling mosquitoes we must think of the natural environment and all its wildlife.

In one large Florida swamp men sprayed the water with poison for three years to kill mosquitoes. But dragonflies, birds, fish and snakes—all mosquito-eaters—were also killed. In the third year more mosquitoes were there than in the first year. It is possible that some mosquitoes get so used to poison that it cannot kill them, but in this case ecologists believe that nature's mosquito controls—insects, birds, fish and snakes—

had kept the mosquitoes down better by eating them than the poison alone could do. The few mosquitoes which escaped the poison at first bred and multiplied in greater numbers than ever, with their natural enemies gone.

In some places it may be necessary to destroy the breeding grounds of mosquitoes by draining marshes and ponds, but draining too many of them may damage the underground water-storage places.

Natural mosquito-eaters which you may see in your own yards and gardens are birds, bats, snakes, spiders, dragonflies and praying mantises. These should not be killed.

Many fish also eat insects, but we have upset the natural relationships of the fish world, too.

Fish take oxygen from water, but in muddy or impure waters they cannot take in enough oxygen to keep them alive. When factories and mines pour waste materials into rivers, when cities dump unpurified sewage there, and when farmers allow soil to run off fields and become mud in nearby streams, they make the water unfit for fish. Water plants which pro-vide food for fish cannot live. Neither can the tiny animals which some fish eat.

53

About fifty years ago, when men began to notice a short-age of fish, they set up fish hatcheries. Here they raised millions of young fish from eggs. Then they turned the young fish loose in streams and lakes. This worked only fairly well, for hatchery fish do not get along well under natural conditions where they have to watch for enemies, bad weather and other dangers to which they are not accustomed. Hatcheries still release full-grown fish in streams where there is much fishing. These fish are usually caught by fishermen very soon.

Ecologists are now studying the different kinds of environments needed by various fish. They believe that if they can improve these environments the number of fish will increase naturally, because the fish will be able to get more of the kind of food they need and better protection from their enemies. An important way to improve stream and lake environments, of course, is to keep soil and waste materials from getting into the water.

Ecologists are also working with the builders of the large dams. They are trying to plan so that the homes of fish and wildlife will not be destroyed when the dams are built. In the great dams of the Columbia River, where the salmon go far upstream to lay their eggs, there are fish ladders to help them over the barriers. These help in salmon conservation.

Other conservationists are working hard to restore our bird life. For many years now it has been against the law for men to shoot birds and sell them to meat markets as food. Laws were passed forbidding this when it was realized that songbirds especially are important insect-eaters.

Some other types of birds are not yet well protected. Some kinds of birds have *all* been killed, or have died because their homes and food were destroyed. You will never see the beautifully colored, graceful passenger pigeons. Less than one hundred years ago there were millions of them in our country. They were killed by the thousands to be sold in markets, and when the forests they needed for food and shelter were destroyed the remaining few died off.

There are only a few whooping cranes left on this continent, but a refuge has been made for them and it is hoped they will increase in number.

Birds like hawks, owls, and eagles have not generally been well protected by laws until recently. It is now illegal to shoot a bald, or American, eagle in the United States. But some useful hawks are still being shot. Birds of this type live mostly by eating small animals or other birds. It used to be thought that they killed many game birds and farmers' chickens. This is not generally true. Ecologists have found that in the long run their eating habits do much more good than harm.

56

There are about fifty species of meadow mouse in North America. One pair of mice may have almost one million descendants in one year. It takes only ten mice to an acre to destroy about five tons of hay in one year. Hawks and owls, which eat many mice, are worth caring for.

Many people are interested in helping birds, and have formed numbers of clubs to protect them. Many of these have joined together in an organization called the National Audubon Society, named for John James Audubon, a famous naturalist and painter of birds. The National Audubon Society and similar organizations have encouraged people to watch birds and study their habits. These bird watchers give scientists much information about the good that birds do and the kind of environments they need.

The National Audubon Society, our state and national governments, and some private citizens have established several hundred wildlife refuges which are used by birds. A refuge is an area set aside for the protection of wildlife. Hunting and other activities which might disturb the wild things or damage their homes and food are forbidden.

Bird clubs, government agents and some private citizens do what is called "birdbanding." The United States Fish and Wildlife Service in the Department of the Interior gives them tiny metal bands and a permit to use them. In banding, the birds are trapped alive in harmless cage traps. A band is fastened to one leg of each bird and the bird is then released. On each band is a number and the words "Return to Department of the Interior, Washington, D. C." Later, if a banded bird is captured or found dead, the finder returns the band to the Department of the Interior, telling when and where he found the bird—often hundreds of miles from where it was banded. By studying the numbers on the bands and the records of where the birds were banded and where they were found, scientists can tell much about how far birds travel and the different environments they inhabit.

By examining the contents of the stomachs of hundreds and hundreds of birds which have died, scientists have learned what each kind eats. In this way they learned that most hawks and owls eat very few farmers' chickens, but a great many mice and rats.

Farmers and homeowners are being encouraged to provide shelter for birds by leaving trees, shrubs or grasses in little-used parts of fields or gardens. Some marshes and ponds are being kept or made to provide breeding places and homes for water birds. Boys and girls can put out birdhouses, bird-feeding trays and bird baths to attract birds to their yards.

Men now protect game birds by law except during certain seasons. These birds—waterfowl like ducks and geese, and land birds like quail, pheasant and grouse—are valued by sportsmen. These men and others recently realized that laws must be passed to prevent game birds, animals and fish from too much hunting. They have helped get game laws passed and they have also helped to set up state and national conservation departments whose job it is to enforce these laws and to build up the numbers of game birds as well as of fish and game animals. These departments are usually supported by money from hunting and fishing licenses. Although not everyone agrees with them, most sportsmen regard game birds and animals as a natural "crop" from which a certain number may be "harvested" each year. With the help of various refuges and of the state and federal conservation departments the numbers of game birds, animals and fish have increased a great deal in some states.

With modern conservation methods many animals that were almost all killed off have been restored to some extent in some regions. By the 1800s the nation's beavers were almost extinct because of the demand for their fur. Their value as conservation animals was not realized. Recently, however, by protecting some of their natural environments and by passing laws against too much trapping, men have helped increase the numbers of beavers greatly. Now, in some places, beavers have to be "managed," because they dam up irrigation ditches or cut down trees in the wrong spots. When this happens, conservation agents trap them alive and move them to other places where their dams will be helpful instead of harmful. Beavers have even been carried in airplanes and dropped into wilderness areas by parachutes. When their specially built box traps hit the ground they break open and the beavers escape to go about their own natural conservation work. Engineers in a few places are actually using beavers for help in flood control along small streams where the floods start.

In North America big game animals like bear, deer, moose, elk, antelope and buffalo were once plentiful. Vast numbers of them were killed for food by pioneers. Finally so few were left that people realized they might die out entirely. Now they are protected by law and their numbers are increasing.

Some animals, deer especially, can find enough food and shelter to get along well, even close to towns, in areas which are partly fields and partly woodlands. In a few states they have increased until there are almost too many for the food supply and some die of starvation during hard winters.

Antelopes have increased so that a little hunting of them is allowed in some states to prevent there being too many for their food supply. Elks have increased recently, also.

Buffaloes, grizzly bears and wolves are still very few. Probably their numbers will not be increased much because there is not enough wild land to support many, and these animals quite easily damage farm crops and ranch stock. A few can be allowed to live, however, in wildlife refuges and in our national forests and parks.

In the heart of our national parks and forests we have some beautiful undamaged spots which show our country as it used to be. Here, where nature is untouched, our conservation specialists can study the relationships of living things. Here, too, our nation's people can have exciting fun.

61

From a high tower on a hill or mountain the fire tower observer watches all day during the season of forest fire danger for signs of smoke or fire. If he sees smoke he looks at it through a sighting instrument which shows him just where the fire is. He at once telephones his fire warden or ranger and they send fire fighters to the fire.

SOME CONSERVATION WORKERS

The forest ranger has charge of a section of our national or state forests. He looks after the welfare of the forest, manages the wild animals, oversees the cutting of trees for lumber, and the protection of the watershed. He works with ranchers whose cattle or sheep are permitted to graze on forest land. He sees that trails and roads are kept up, gets new trees planted where needed, and helps enforce the game laws.

The fire warden is in charge of forest fire protection in local areas. He may be appointed by the federal, state or local government. If you should see a forest fire starting, ask a telephone operator to connect you with the fire warden and report the fire.

A biologist may work for the United States Fish and Wildlife Service, a state conservation department, or a conservation organization. He may study the way fish and animals live. He may count the number of fish in a stream or study the stomach contents of killed animals to see what they eat. He may observe everything a certain animal such as a beaver does, in order to collect facts that will help in improving its living conditions.

A game protector must catch and bring to trial people who break the laws that prevent killing too many animals or fish. He also may study the way animals and fish live in his region and try to improve their habitat so that their numbers will increase.

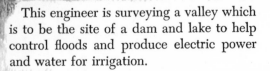

This engineer is surveying a valley which is to be the site of a dam and lake to help control floods and produce electric power and water for irrigation.

63

WHAT YOU CAN DO

YOU do not have to go to a great national park or forest to see nature at work, however. In your own yard and garden or in the small park near your home nature's giving and taking is there to watch. That downy woodpecker drilling on a tree is not digging a hole just to harm the tree. It is getting food. That swallow darting and swooping every which way is not crazy. It is catching insects in the air.

You can watch the birds, the insects, the animals and the plants growing, living and working together. When you see a robin on the lawn, a zinnia in the garden, a muskrat in the stream, a crow in the cornfield, try to figure out what each one is giving and what each is taking.

You can think out your place in nature, too. What are

your relations with other living things? How do you fit into their scheme, and how do they affect your life?

In many ways you yourself can be a conservationist. The pictures on pages 66-67 give some suggestions. You can think of others.

There are many, many things that even scientists do not yet know about the relations of plants and animals to us and their environments. And there are many things they do not know about ways to help plants and animals work for the greatest good to them and to us.

If you like to watch the interesting, exciting lives of nature, perhaps you may be one to find the answers to some of the questions. At least you will have the fun of looking and of puzzling out the fascinating ways in which nature's jigsaw pattern of giving and taking fits together.

YOU AND CONSERVATION

Leave bird nests alone until you are sure the eggs have hatched and both young and old birds have gone from the nest for the season.

If the fish you catch is too small to eat, throw it back quickly into the water so that it may have a chance to grow bigger. Do not keep more fish than you can use.

Learn the names of the rare wildflowers which should not be picked in your region. Some states have laws that prevent the picking of certain flowers or the digging up of certain plants.

66

Learn what are the useful insects in your community, and let them live.

Put up a bird house in your yard.

Remember never to cut living trees with knife or ax. Never carve initials on a tree.

Plant grass or other plant cover in places on your yard or farm where water washes soil away.

CONSERVATION TERMS

CONSERVATION—the protecting, renewing or increasing of our land, water, plant, wildlife and mineral resources.

CONTOUR PLOWING—plowing which follows the contours, or naturally equal points of height across a slope, and so prevents rain from washing away topsoil.

ECOLOGY—the study of the relationships of plants and animals with each other and with their environment. A worker in ecology is an *ecologist*.

EROSION—the wearing away of natural materials. This word is often used in describing the washing away of land by water.

FOOD CHAIN—the relationships in which plants and animals are linked because they depend on one another for food.

LAND-USE MAP—a detailed map of an area, showing how it may best be treated in order to conserve and increase its resources.

NATURAL ENVIRONMENT—all the natural things and conditions that surround a plant or animal . . . its natural surroundings.

NATURAL RESOURCES—the soil, water, plants, animals, minerals and any other supplies furnished by nature.

PLANT COVER—the covering of plants which protects the soil's surface.

ROTATION PLANTING—the process of varying, in a planned and definite order, the crops grown on a piece of ground.

WATERSHED—a ridge and its slopes down which water flows to drainage valleys.

WATER TABLE—the topmost level reached by the water stored naturally underground.

OTHER BOOKS TO READ

Shippen, Katherine B.—Great Heritage—The Viking Press, 1949.

Van Dersal, William Richard and E. H. Graham—Land Renewed; the Story of Soil Conservation—Oxford University Press, 1946.

INDEX